JOURNEY THROUGH A BOOK

Written by Heather Croft

Illustrations created with AI

Heather Croft Books
First Published 2023, Ventura, CA
Copyright © Heather Croft Parks

All rights Reserved

No part of this publication can be reproduced or transmitted in any form or by any means of mechanical, electronic, photocopying, recording or otherwise without the written permission of the publisher

Dedication

For Emily – my forever joy and always inspiration.

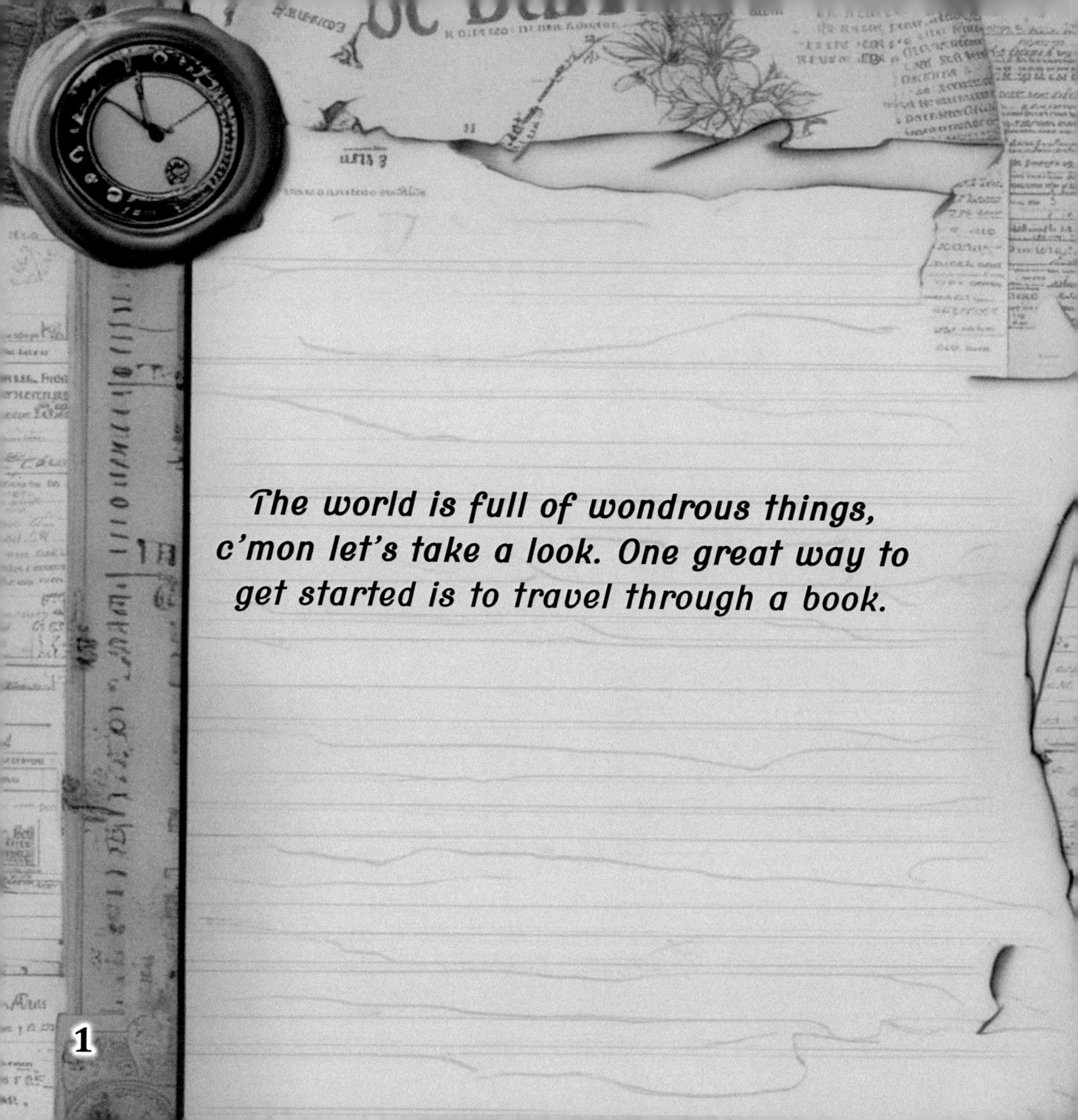

The world is full of wondrous things, c'mon let's take a look. One great way to get started is to travel through a book.

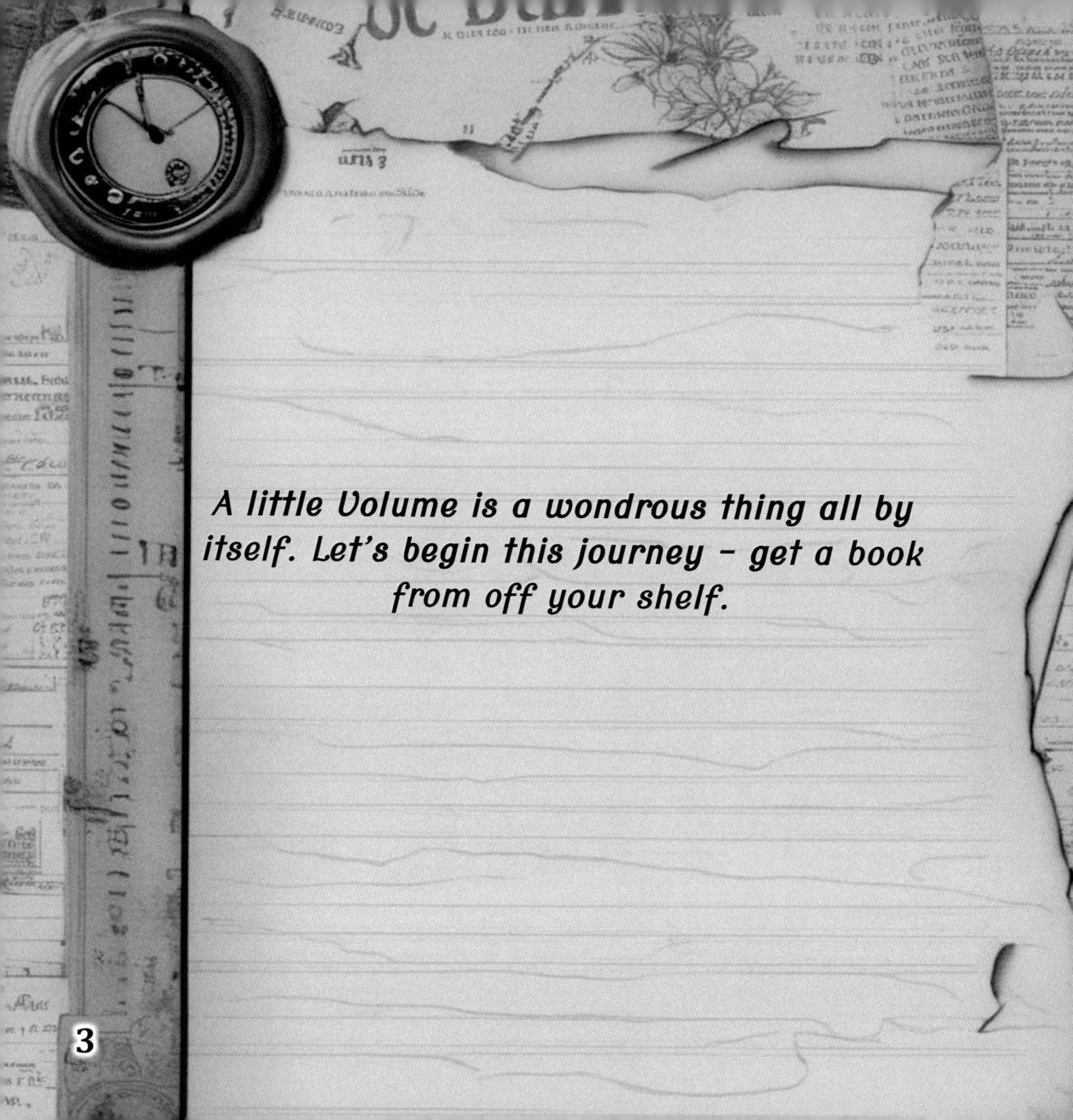

A little Volume is a wondrous thing all by itself. Let's begin this journey – get a book from off your shelf.

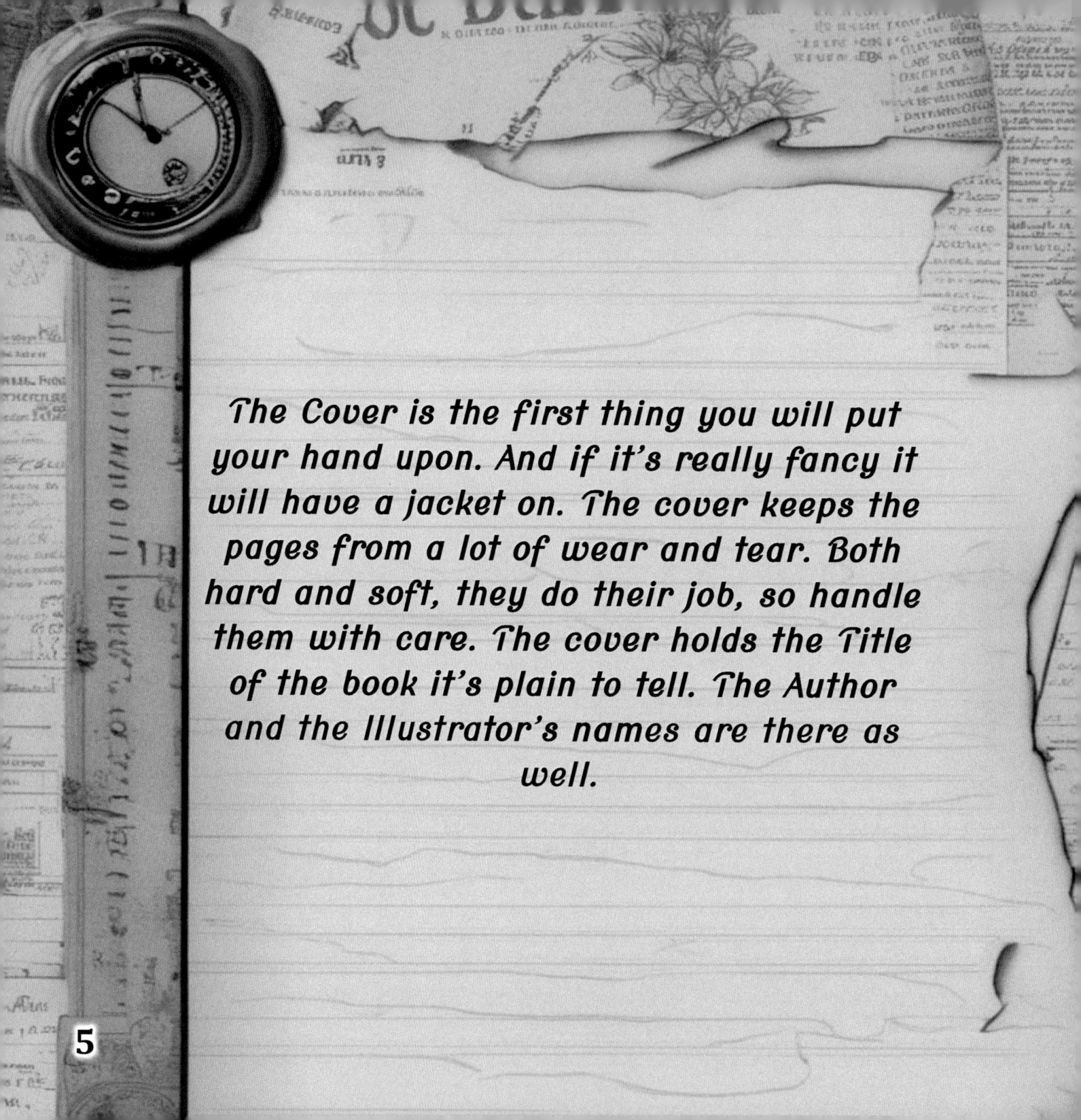

The Cover is the first thing you will put your hand upon. And if it's really fancy it will have a jacket on. The cover keeps the pages from a lot of wear and tear. Both hard and soft, they do their job, so handle them with care. The cover holds the Title of the book it's plain to tell. The Author and the Illustrator's names are there as well.

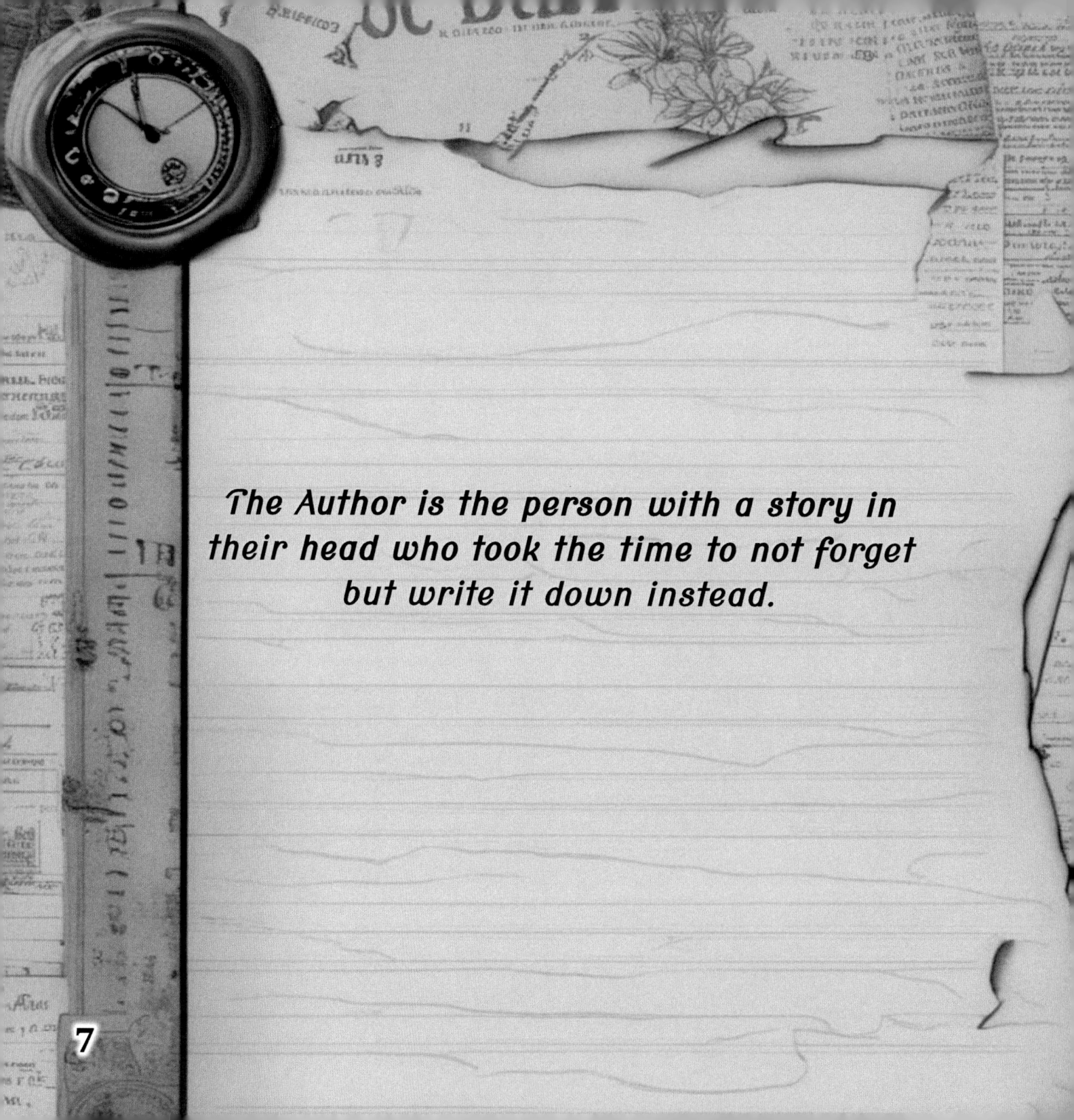

The Author is the person with a story in their head who took the time to not forget but write it down instead.

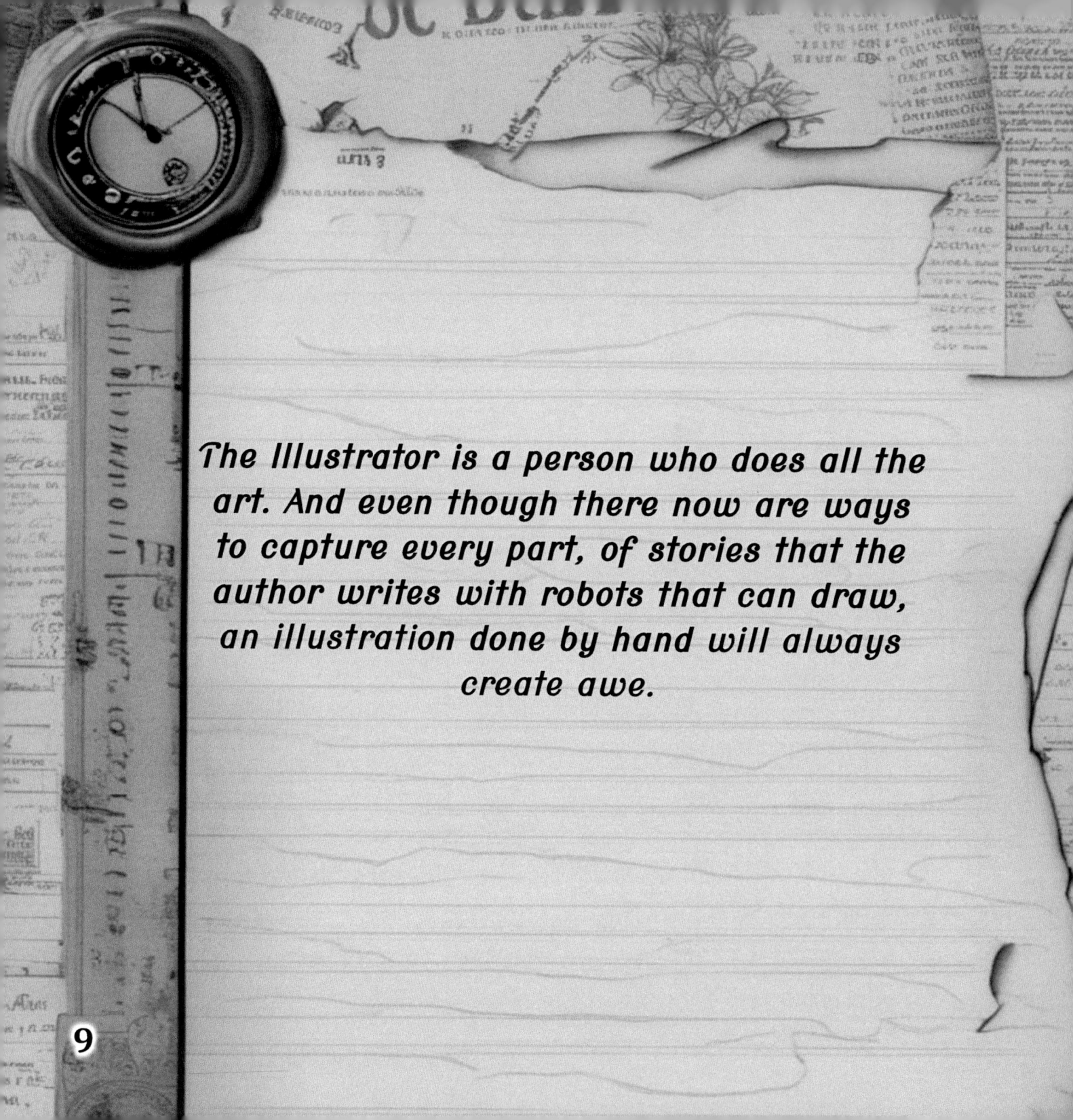

The Illustrator is a person who does all the art. And even though there now are ways to capture every part, of stories that the author writes with robots that can draw, an illustration done by hand will always create awe.

10

The Spine of any book runs down the back just like your own. It's where the pages of a book are glued, stapled or sewn.

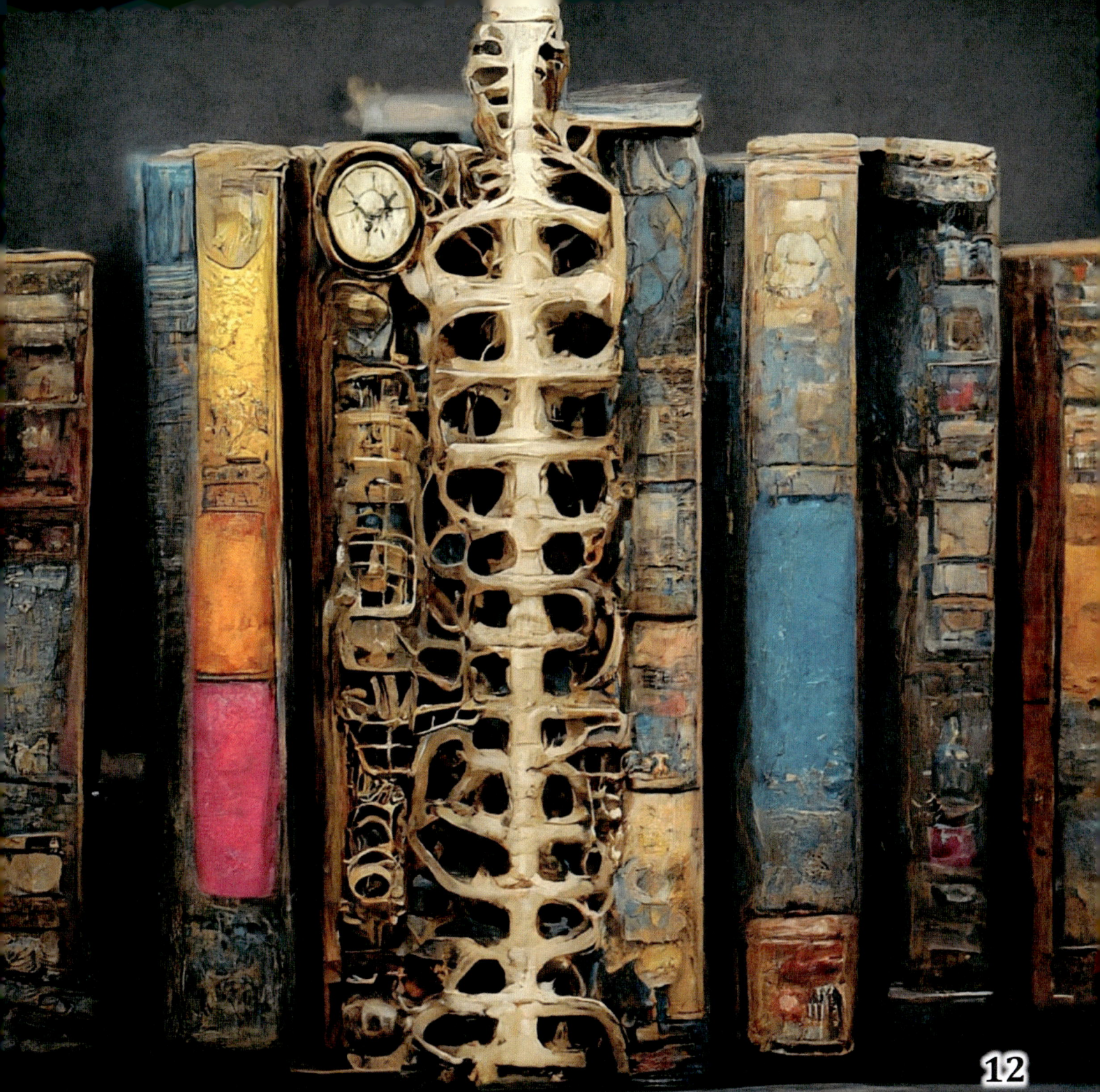

The reason that the pages must be gathered in this way is that if they were not, you might be chasing them all day!

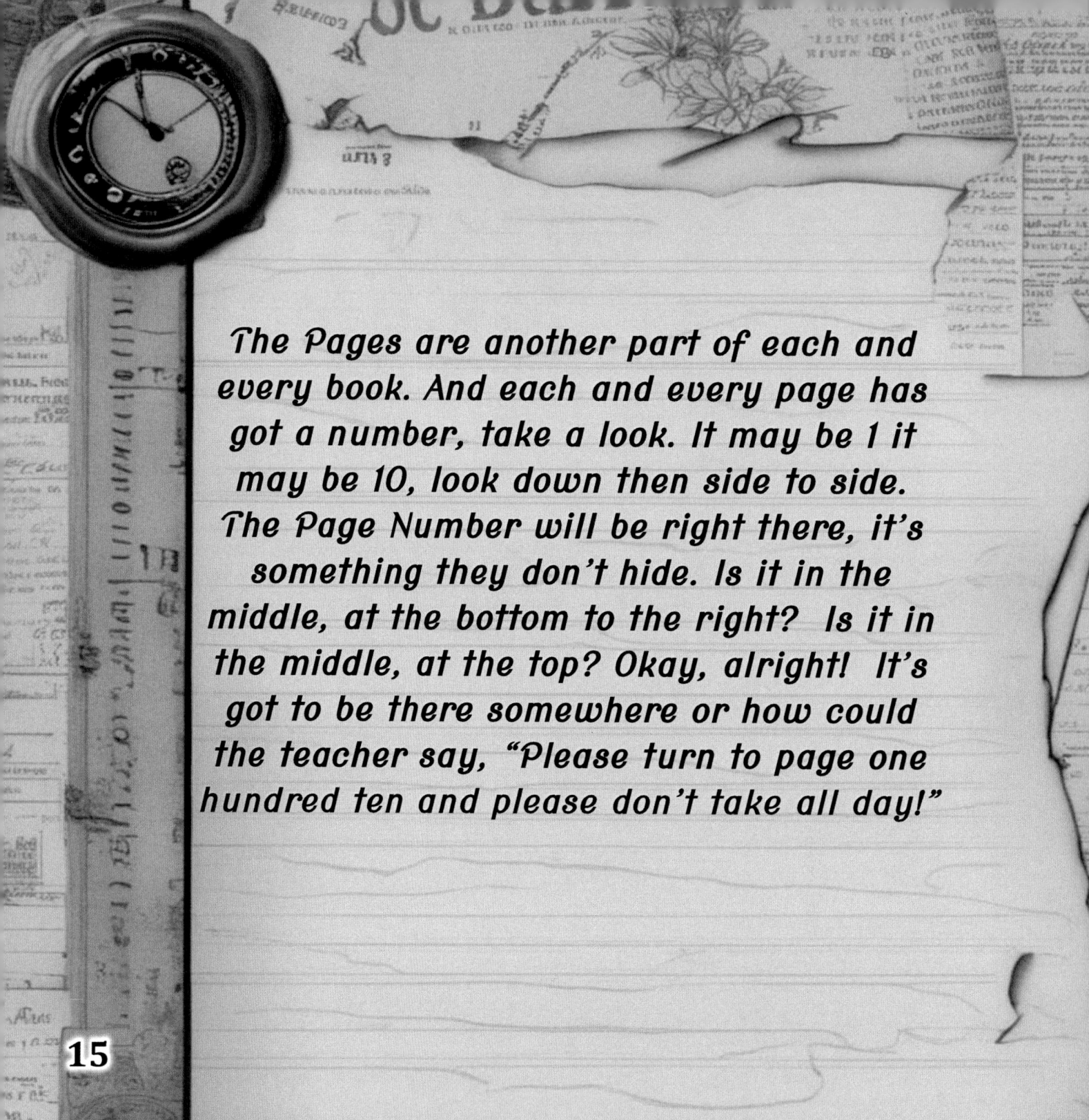

The Pages are another part of each and every book. And each and every page has got a number, take a look. It may be 1 it may be 10, look down then side to side. The Page Number will be right there, it's something they don't hide. Is it in the middle, at the bottom to the right? Is it in the middle, at the top? Okay, alright! It's got to be there somewhere or how could the teacher say, "Please turn to page one hundred ten and please don't take all day!"

Just open up the cover and you'll see a Title Page which tells us what the cover did then adds another stage. More helpful information like the Publisher and where the publisher prints all the books then ships them out from there.

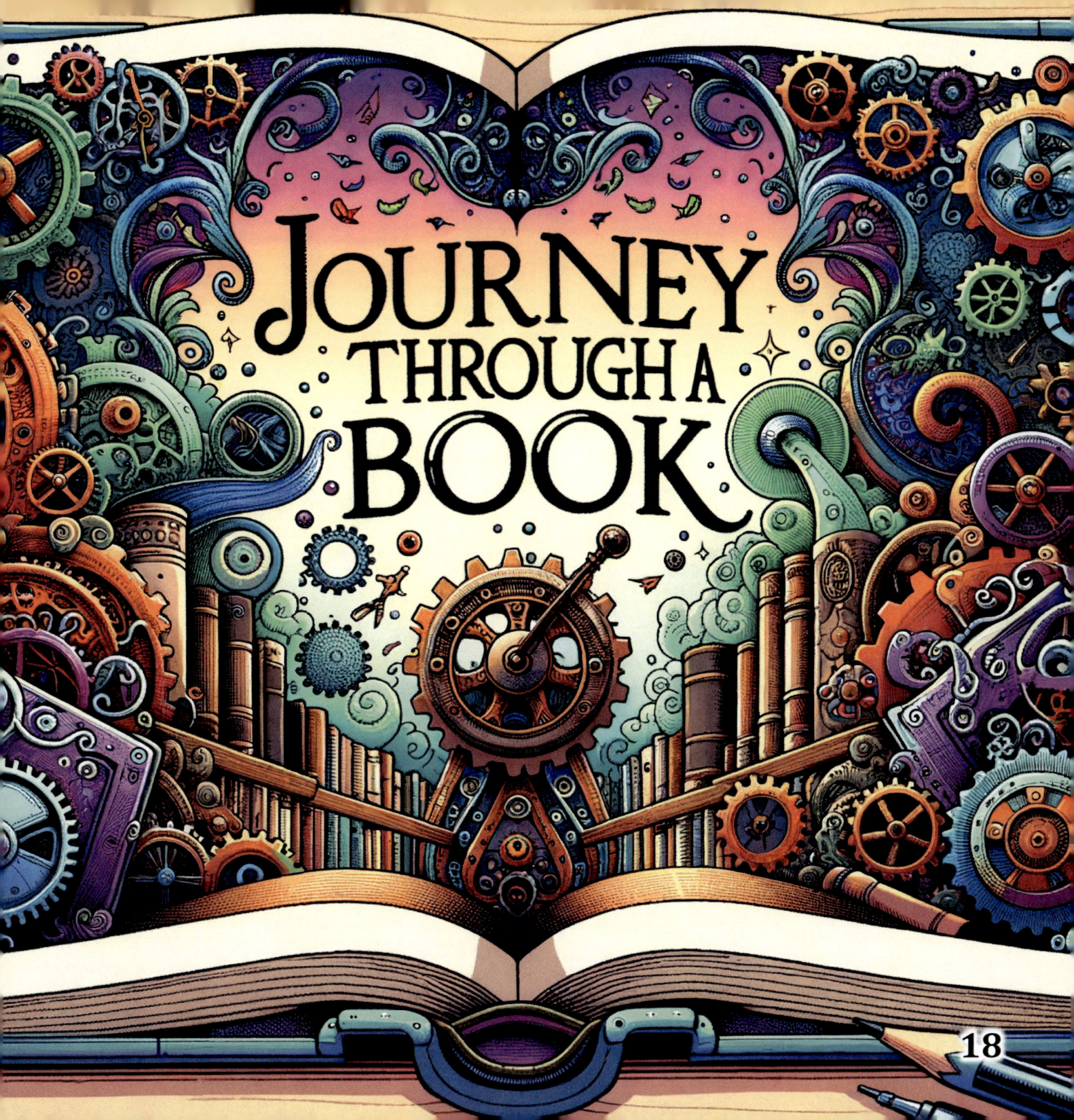

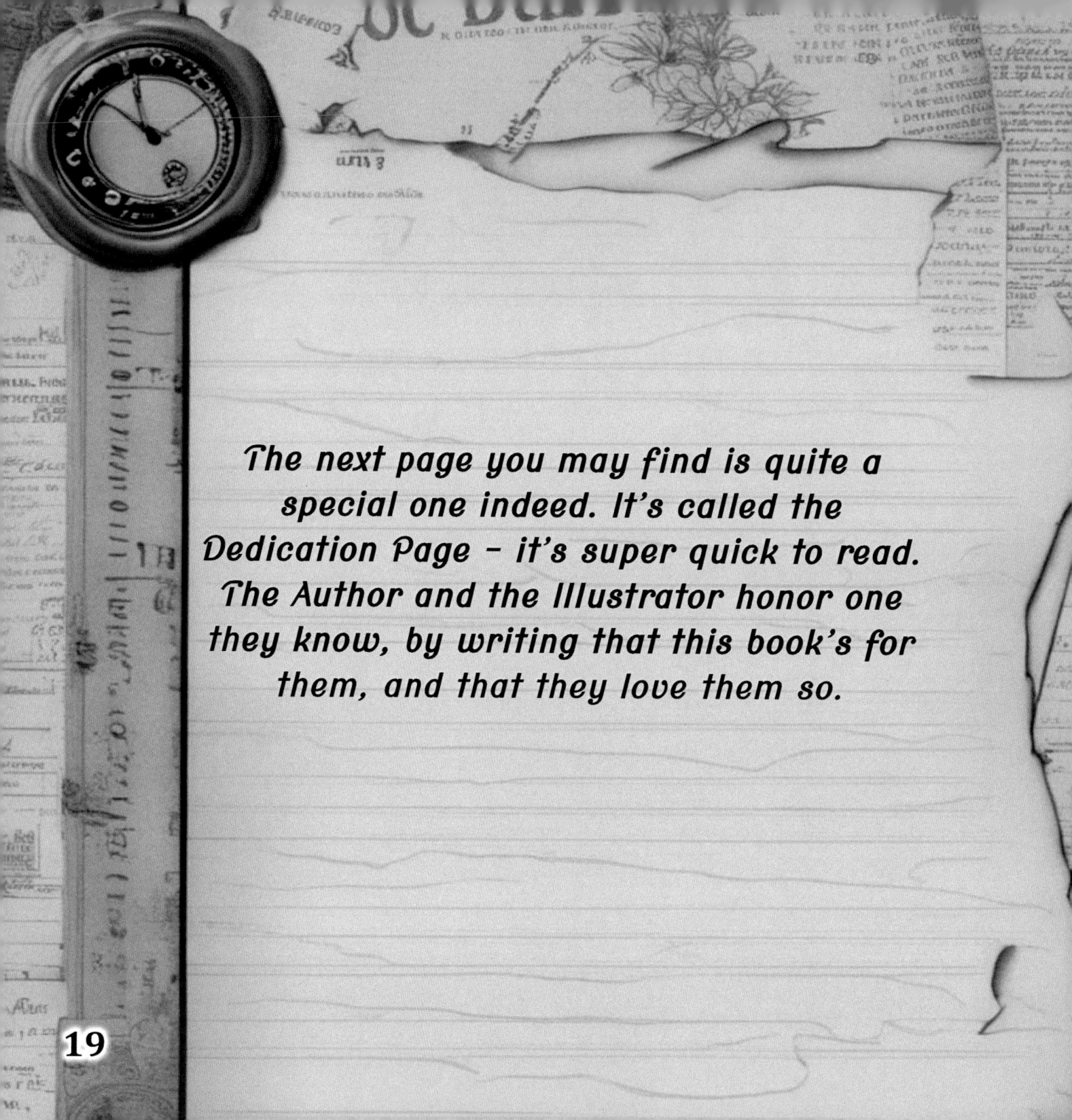

The next page you may find is quite a special one indeed. It's called the Dedication Page – it's super quick to read. The Author and the Illustrator honor one they know, by writing that this book's for them, and that they love them so.

There is another page and it is different from the rest. It is a page called by its name and holds a special list. This list is called a "Table" and it shows the "Contents Of" the book that you are reading, perhaps one you'll come to love. The Chapters line up on the left, Page Numbers on the right. This way you'll find out what's inside before you take all night to read and read then realize this book's not right at all. You need a book about spring and this one's about fall!

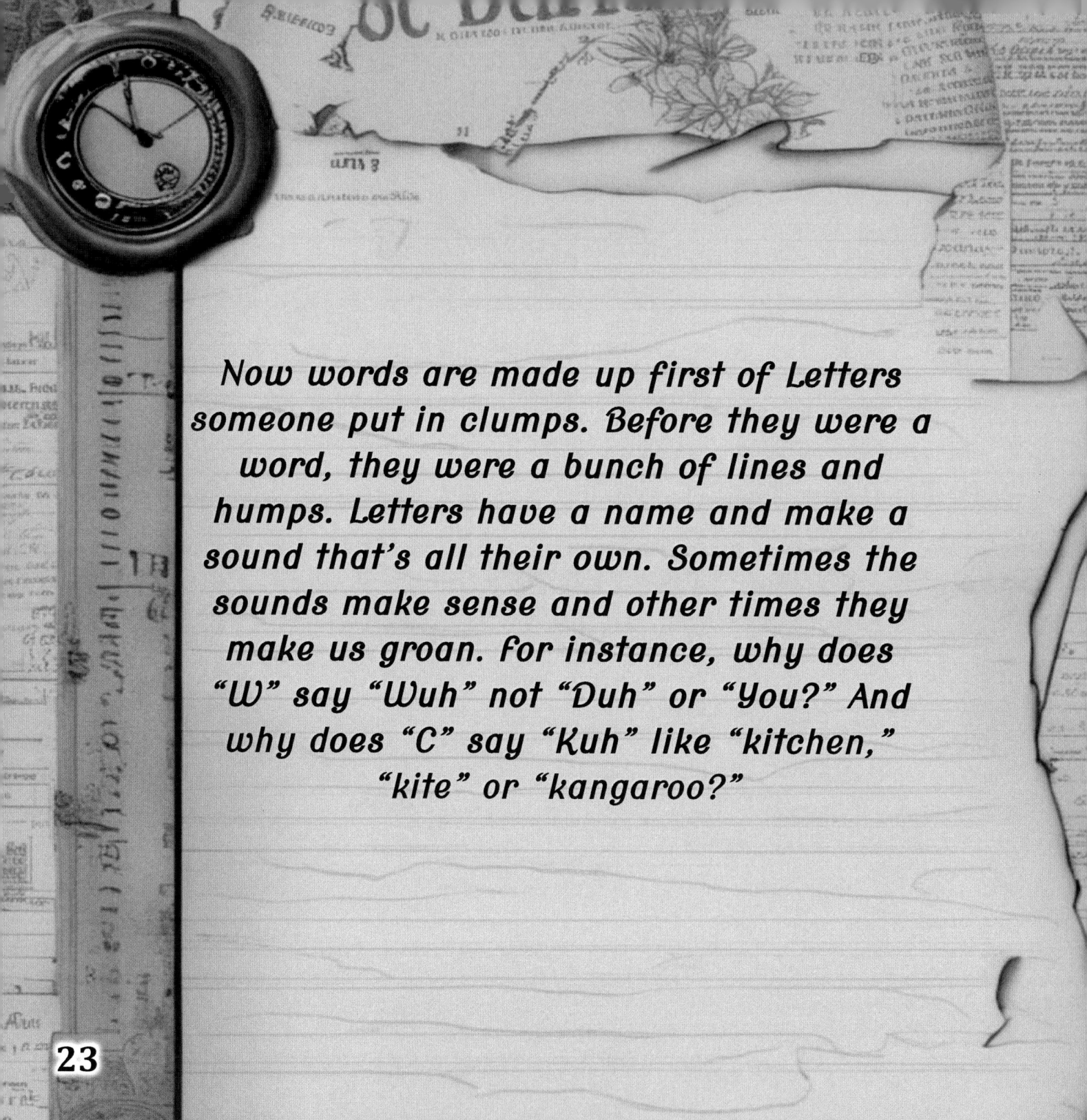

Now words are made up first of Letters someone put in clumps. Before they were a word, they were a bunch of lines and humps. Letters have a name and make a sound that's all their own. Sometimes the sounds make sense and other times they make us groan. for instance, why does "W" say "Wuh" not "Duh" or "You?" And why does "C" say "Kuh" like "kitchen," "kite" or "kangaroo?"

Our ABC's are Consonants and Vowels, they're split in two. The consonants are everything but A, E, I, O, U.

And A, E, I, O, U are very busy, yes indeed.
At least one vowel must be inside of every
word we read.

Now speaking of the English words they go from left to right. Your eyes must move the same way too or there's a chance you might start reading some things backward and that is not good because you read a word like "saw" that way and it will come out "was."

In many languages the Letters go from right to left. Or up or down, read down to up, the writers are quite deft! These letters look like artwork and they bring us joy to see, the way we all communicate with such diversity!

A Sentence is a group of words, they sit upon one line. They tell about one main idea then make that idea shine. The Subject is that main idea, the Predicate's the rest. for instance you'd say "Cats are fun and like to sleep the best." The subject would be "cats" of course, the predicate comes next to tell us other details about cats right in the text.

Cats are fun and like to sleep the best.

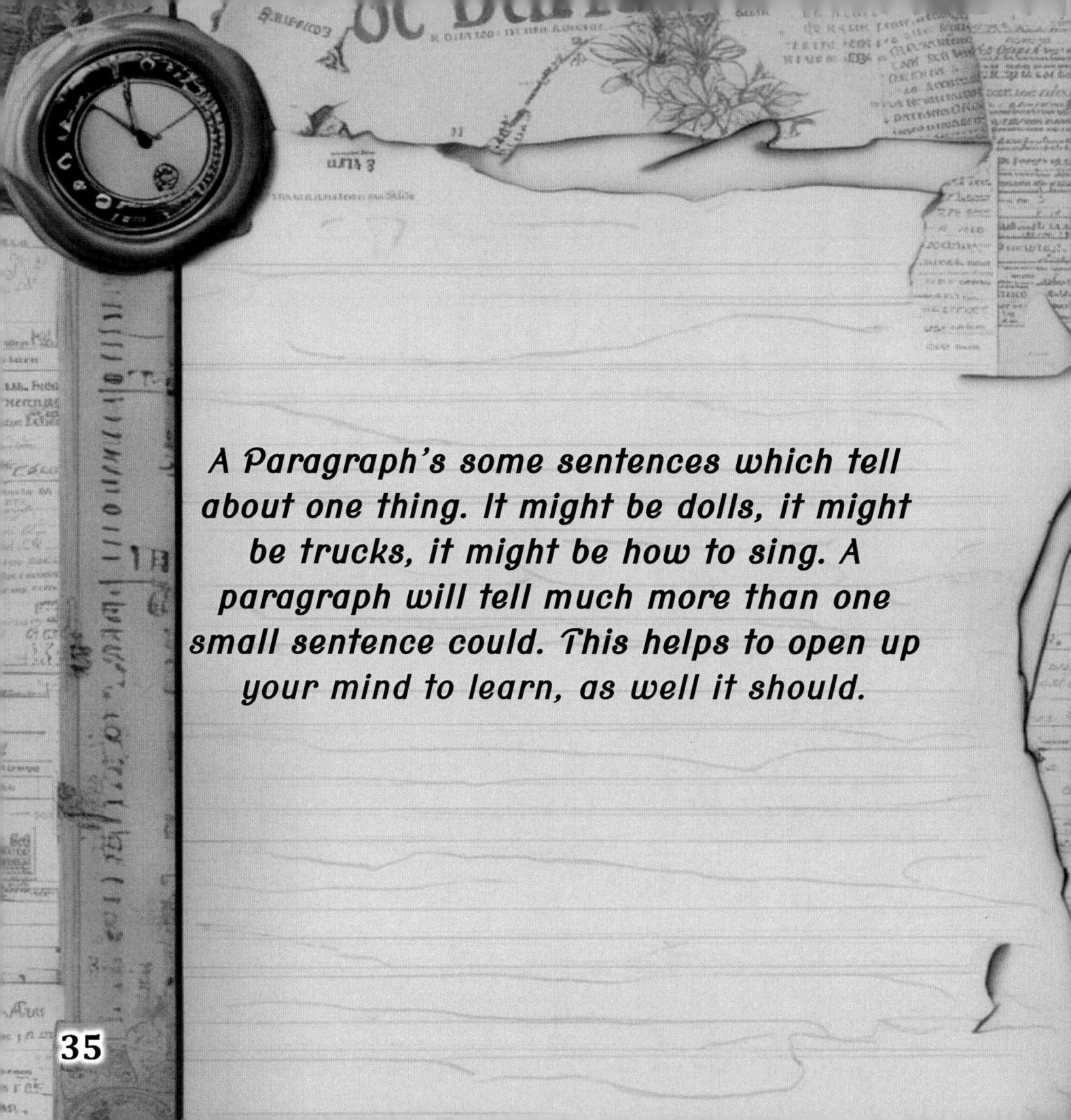

A Paragraph's some sentences which tell about one thing. It might be dolls, it might be trucks, it might be how to sing. A paragraph will tell much more than one small sentence could. This helps to open up your mind to learn, as well it should.

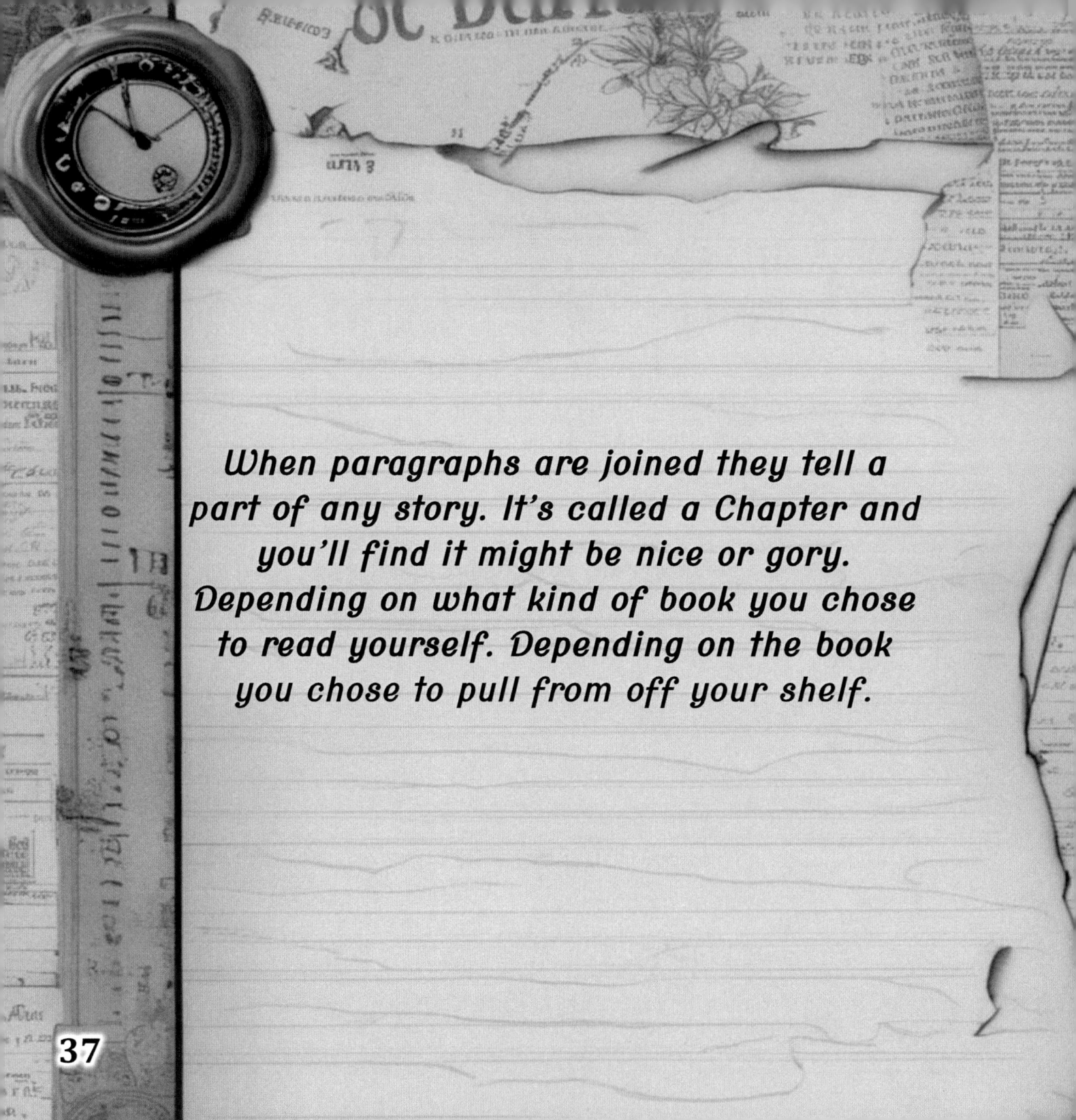

When paragraphs are joined they tell a part of any story. It's called a Chapter and you'll find it might be nice or gory. Depending on what kind of book you chose to read yourself. Depending on the book you chose to pull from off your shelf.

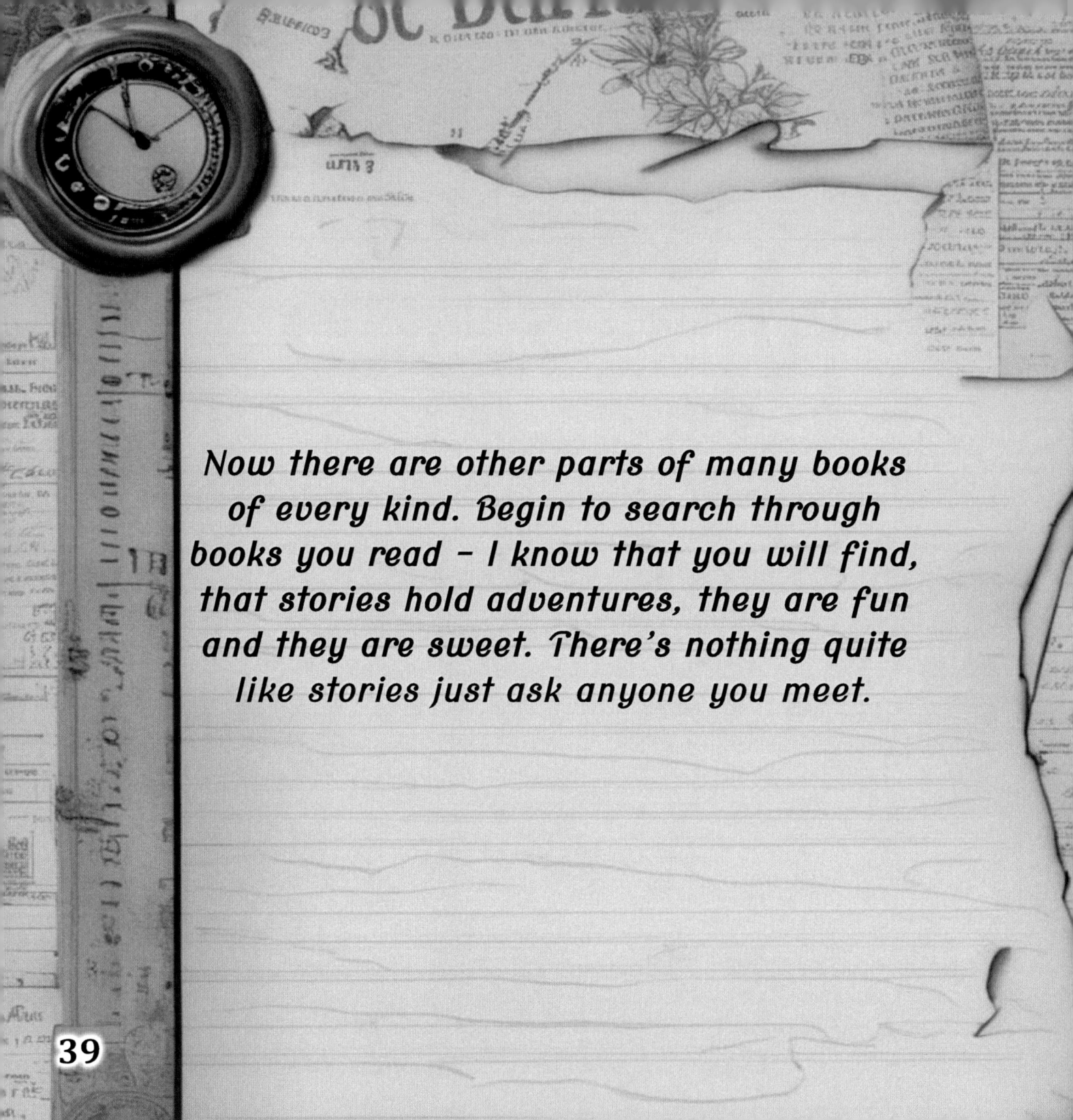

Now there are other parts of many books of every kind. Begin to search through books you read – I know that you will find, that stories hold adventures, they are fun and they are sweet. There's nothing quite like stories just ask anyone you meet.

Scan this QR Code for a downloadable book template.

Made in the USA
Middletown, DE
08 October 2025